# Gordon Korman

## Sheelagh Matthews

www.av2books.com

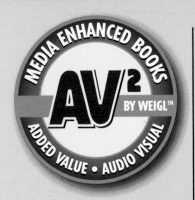

AV² provides enriched content that supplements and complements this book. Weigl's AV² books strive to create inspired learning and engage young minds in a total learning experience.

## Your AV² Media Enhanced books come alive with...

**Audio**
Listen to sections of the book read aloud.

**Key Words**
Study vocabulary, and complete a matching word activity.

**Video**
Watch informative video clips.

**Quizzes**
Test your knowledge.

**Embedded Weblinks**
Gain additional information for research.

**Slide Show**
View images and captions, and prepare a presentation.

**Try This!**
Complete activities and hands-on experiments.

**... and much, much more!**

Go to **www.av2books.com,** and enter this book's unique code.

**BOOK CODE**

**D 7 4 5 3 4 7**

**AV² by Weigl** brings you media enhanced books that support active learning.

Published by AV² by Weigl
350 5th Avenue, 59th Floor
New York, NY 10118
USA
Website: www.weigl.com          www.av2books.com

Library of Congress Cataloging-in-Publication Data

Matthews, Sheelagh.
  Gordon Korman/Sheelagh Matthews.
    p. cm. -- (Remarkable writers)
  Includes index.
  ISBN 978-1-61913-055-5 (hard cover : alk. paper) -- ISBN 978-1-61913-597-0 (soft cover : alk. paper) -- ISBN 978-1-61913-720-2 (ebook)
  1. Korman, Gordon--Juvenile literature. 2. Authors, American--20th century--Biography--Juvenile literature. 3. Children's stories--Authorship--Juvenile literature. I. Title.
  PS3561.O3398Z75 2013
  813'.54--dc23
  [B]
                                        2012003161

Printed in the United States of America, in North Mankato, Minnesota
1 2 3 4 5 6 7 8 9 0  16 15 14 13 12

062012
WEP170512

Senior Editor: Heather Kissock
Design: Terry Paulhus

Weigl acknowledges Getty Images as its primary photo supplier for this title.
Scholastic Inc./Scholastic Press: pages 5 (SJI Associates), 7, 10 (Everest: Book one - The Contest cover photograph by Earl Robicheaux), 10 (Dive: Book one - The Discovery cover photograph by Kelly La Duke), 13 (I Want to Go Home cover photograph by Rodrigo Moreno), 13 (Jake Reinvented cover photograph by Uwe Krejci/Getty Images), 13 (SJI Associates),18 (SJI Associates), 20 (JoAnne Ainolfi), 21 (Showoff jacket art by Jennifer Taylor).

# Contents

# Introducing Gordon Korman

Gordon Korman says he knew writing was the career for him by his senior year of high school. By then, he had written and **published** four books and was working on a fifth. Gordon is the author of the popular Bruno and Boots series of books, which is set in a boarding school for boys. This award-winning and best-selling author has been writing books to entertain children and youth since he was only 12 years old.

"There's always a little bit of real life behind my storylines."
—*Gordon Korman*

Gordon's ability to relate to children on their terms, using funny circumstances and unforgettable characters, makes his writing a hit with young audiences around the world. He has written more than 70 books that have sold more than 7 million copies over three decades, proving that kids love his fast-paced, zany humor and wild imagination. Luckily for his avid readers, it seems Gordon Korman always has a new book coming out.

The Bruno and Boots series takes place in a boarding school. This is a school where children live as well as learn.

Most of Gordon's early books were comedies, sometimes based on his own life. Later, his writing shifted to adventure and action, with stories full of suspense and mystery. This led to an invitation to be a part of the writing team for a brand new concept in books, an interactive action series called The 39 Clues. Always seeking new challenges, Gordon then took up writing historical fiction. He has even co-written two books of poetry with his mother. This young-at-heart writer loves to return to schools on author visits and reading tours.

The first novel in The 39 Clues series, *The Maze of Bones*, was released in 2008.

Writers are often inspired to record the stories of people who lead interesting lives. The story of another person's life is known as a biography. A biography can tell the story of any person, from authors such as Gordon Korman, to inventors, presidents, and sports stars.

When writing a biography, authors must first collect information about their subject. This information may come from a book about the person's life, a news article about one of his or her accomplishments, or a review of his or her work. Libraries and the internet will have much of this information. Most biographers will also interview their subjects. Personal accounts provide a great deal of information and a unique point of view. When some basic details about the person's life have been collected, it is time to begin writing a biography.

As you read about Gordon Korman, you will be introduced to the important parts of a biography. Use these tips, and the examples provided, to learn how to write about an author or any other remarkable person.

# Early Life

**G**ordon Korman was born on October 23, 1963, in Montreal, Quebec and raised in Toronto, Ontario, Canada. His father was an accountant, and his mother, Bernice, wrote a humorous **column** for a local newspaper. Gordon was named after Gordie Howe, a well-known hockey player.

"I didn't know any publishing companies, and I think that's why I ended up with Scholastic. At the time, I was the class monitor for Scholastic book orders, so I'm thinking 'I'm practically an employee of these guys already.' So I mailed my **manuscript** to the address on the book order forms."
—*Gordon Korman*

An only child, Gordon amused himself with writing from a very early age. In elementary school, he would take a creative angle with his schoolwork whenever possible. When it was time to write all the week's spelling words in a sentence, Gordon would come up with the silliest and funniest sentences he could imagine.

✍ Gordie Howe is considered one of the best hockey players of all time. In 2008, he received the first Lifetime Achievement Award ever given by the National Hockey League.

A seventh grade English project started Gordon's writing career. When his school had a shortage of English teachers, Gordon's track and field coach, Mr. Hamilton, was given the job. The coach did not have much experience with teaching English and gave the class a semester-long writing assignment. Each school day from February to June, Gordon had a whole class period to work on writing. He invented the characters Bruno and Boots, two troublemaking boys who were doing their best to survive life in the rule-filled world of a private boys' school. His efforts earned him an A+ for the story, but his final mark was downgraded to a B+ because his work was messy.

In middle school, Gordon was the monitor for his school's Scholastic Arrow Book Club. One day, he mailed the manuscript from his English assignment to Scholastic at the address on the Arrow book order form. Two years later, in 1978, Scholastic published his book. Gordon was only 14 years old. The publication of *This Can't Be Happening at Macdonald Hall!* began a writing career for Gordon that would span decades. He dedicated his first book to Mr. Hamilton, the teacher responsible for that semester of writing.

A person's early years have a strong influence on his or her future. Parents, teachers, and friends can have a large impact on how a person thinks, feels, and behaves. These effects are strong enough to last throughout childhood, and often a person's lifetime.

In order to write about a person's early life, biographers must find answers to the following questions.

**1** Where and when was the person born?

**2** What is known about the person's family and friends?

**3** Did the person grow up in unusual circumstances?

GORDON KORMAN

This CAN'T Be HAPPENING at Macdonald Hall!

SCHOLASTIC

At first, Gordon's books were sold only through book clubs. They were not available in bookstores until later.

# Growing Up

Gordon did most of his growing up in Thornhill, Ontario, a suburb of Toronto. He attended German Mills Public School and completed high school at Thornlea Secondary School. His writing career flourished while he was in high school, and his teachers and classmates took his success in stride. His friends handled his increasing **celebrity** well. They understood that writing was just something that he was good at, just like others might be good at sports.

"When I was in the sixth grade I was the G-Man. I loved it. I've been waiting 25 years to get another nickname that good."
—*Gordon Korman*

Gordon was 17 years old when he was given the Air Canada Award for the Most Promising Writer Under 35 by the Canadian Authors Association. He had been writing one book a year since his success with his best-selling first book. He would write these books while on vacation from school.

## Get to Know Ontario

CANADA

Minnesota

Lake Superior

Ontario

Quebec

Wisconsin

Lake Huron

UNITED STATES

Thornhill • ☆Toronto

Lake Ontario

Michigan

New York

Lake Michigan

Iowa

Lake Erie

Illinois

Pennsylvania

**ONTARIO MAP LEGEND**

☐ Ontario
☆ Capital City
☐ Canada
☐ United States
☐ State Borders
☐ Water

100 Miles
SCALE 0
100 Kilometers

Scholastic published four books by the young author while Gordon was still in high school. He wrote the kinds of stories that he himself wanted to read but could not find when he was a youth. Gordon started writing before the age of personal computers, so he would first write his stories in longhand, then type them out on a typewriter.

Gordon shares some of his own life experiences through a few of his characters. Zoe, from *Liar, Liar, Pants on Fire*, is full of imaginative excuses and exaggerations, just as Gordon was. Gordon describes himself as a cowardly Bruno from his *Bruno and Boots* series. While Bruno and Gordon both like to plan mischievous schemes, Gordon lacked the courage to carry them out. Bruno, on the other hand, has no such fear.

Like his namesake, Gordie Howe, Gordon's favorite sport was hockey. He even wrote a series of books about hockey, called *Slapshots*. Gordie Howe had a nickname, *Mr. Hockey*. Gordon loved the idea of having a nickname, too, but was disappointed by the boring nicknames he was given, like Gord-o or Gordie. His cool nickname finally came when someone called him the *G-Man*, and it stuck.

# Writing About
## Growing Up

Some people know what they want to achieve in life from a very young age. Others do not decide until much later. In any case, it is important for biographers to discuss when and how their subjects make these decisions. Using the information they collect, biographers try to answer the following questions about their subjects' paths in life.

**1** Who had the most influence on the person?

**2** Did he or she receive assistance from others?

**3** Did the person have a positive attitude?

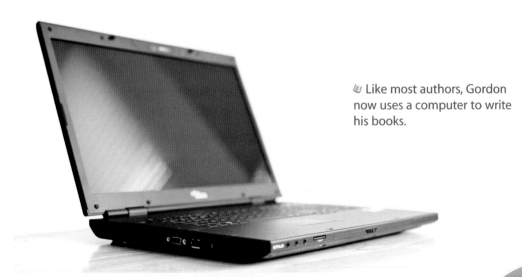

📖 Like most authors, Gordon now uses a computer to write his books.

# Developing Skills

As Gordon grew older and more experienced, his writing evolved. His books could always be found under **juvenile fiction** in the library, but he wrote for both children and young adults (YA). Gordon finds writing for younger children difficult. He believes it takes children until third or fourth grade to perceive humor and understand character development.

"When I was two years old, I wanted to be a dog when I grew up. I don't actually remember this, but my parents tell me that I used to eat dinner under the table in preparation for this career."
—Gordon Korman

Although he was best known for writing comedy, Gordon has been willing to take on new writing challenges throughout his career. He began to write action and adventure stories based partly on events that happened in real life. Some of these stories required extensive **research**, such as the books in the *Dive, Everest,* and *Island* series. His books in the *Titanic* series were based on historical facts about the doomed ship. Gordon had a hard time writing the *Titanic* series, as he loves happy endings. The sinking of a mighty ship from hitting an iceberg is not a happy ending.

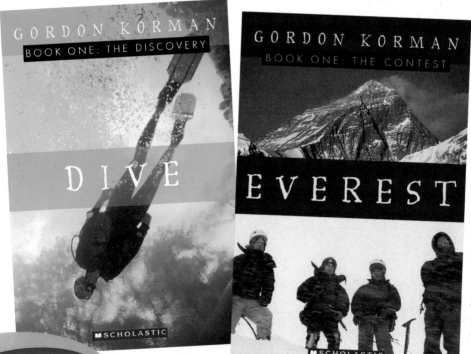

The *Dive* and *Everest* series are written for teenagers.

Gordon learned to use real experiences as a springboard for his imagination. He also discovered that the power of observation was important to good writing, especially in conveying humor. Gordon creates characters that live between regular life and the world of excitement and fantasy. The trick, he explains, is to be able to move smoothly from one realm to the other. Sometimes, he says, his characters become like real people, and it feels like they help him write his books.

Gordon believes that ideas become better when they are shared. He talks about his story ideas with friends to get them out into the open and to get feedback. Sometimes, his ideas will take off, but sometimes he finds out that the ideas he thought were amazing really were not that great.

For books like those in the *Dive*, *Everest*, and *Titanic* series, Gordon learned to research. He knew nothing about diving or climbing Everest before he started those books. He knew that the *Titanic* sank, but he had to learn much more about the ship and the **culture** of 1912 before he could write the book.

# Writing About Developing Skills

Every remarkable person has skills and traits that make him or her noteworthy. Some people have natural talent, while others practice diligently. For most, it is a combination of the two. One of the most important things that a biographer can do is to tell the story of how their subject developed his or her talents.

**1** What was the person's education?

**2** What was the person's first job or work experience?

**3** What obstacles did the person overcome?

The *Titanic* was believed to be unsinkable. However, it sank to the floor of the Atlantic Ocean in 1912 after hitting an iceberg on its maiden voyage.

# Timeline of Gordon Korman

### 1985
Gordon graduates with a Bachelor of Fine Arts degree from New York University (NYU).

### 1963
Gordon Korman is born on October 23 in Montreal, Quebec, Canada.

AIR CANADA

### 1981
Gordon wins the Canadian Authors Association (CAA) Air Canada Award for Most Promising Writer Under 35.

### 1976
At age 12, Gordon writes his first book, *This Can't Be Happening At Macdonald Hall!*, for a seventh grade school project.

### SCHOLASTIC

### 1978
*This Can't Be Happening At Macdonald Hall!* is published by Scholastic.

## 2004

*Jake, Reinvented*, a book about a mysterious new student, wins the American Library Association (ALA) Award for Best Book for Young Adults.

## 2008

*The 39 Clues: One False Note* is published. It is Gordon's first novel in the adventure series.

## 1986

*I Want to Go Home!*, about a boy sent to an athletic camp against his will, wins the International Reading Association (IRA) Children's Choice Award.

## 2001

Gordon shifts from writing humor to action/adventure with the *Island* series.

## 1996

Gordon creates a fictional author named Jerry Bloom and co-writes a poetry book by "Jeremy Bloom" with his mother, Bernice Korman. The book is entitled *The Last-Place Sports Poems of Jeremy Bloom: A Collection of Poems About Winning, Losing, and Being a Good Sport (Sometimes).*

# Early Achievements

A s a young man, Gordon set off to New York to study film and dramatic writing. In 1985, he received his Bachelor of Fine Arts (BFA) degree from New York University (NYU). Many of his friends at NYU did not realize that Gordon was a writer. By the time he graduated from high school, he had already published a number of titles, including *Beware the Fish, Losing Joe's Place,* and *Go Jump in the Pool.* When his friends were on school break, Gordon would be on book tours. He hardly ever talked about his writing life with his friends because he was afraid to sound **conceited**.

"I try to make my characters funny and/or exciting because writing a novel is almost like living with those characters for a few months."
—*Gordon Korman*

📖 Founded in 1831, NYU is one of the largest private, nonprofit universities in the United States.

Gordon published five books while attending NYU, including *The War with Mr. Wizzle*, *I Want to Go Home*, and *No Coins, Please*. He found that his writing improved with practice. Gordon also learned that enthusiasm and keen powers of observation were good skills for a writer to have. Writing in different ways helped Gordon hone his skills as well.

Gordon has written several **screenplays**, but so far none have been made into films. However, his writing has still made it to the screen in other ways. The Disney Channel turned Gordon's *Monday Night Football* book series into a television show. These stories featured a sports jersey with superpowers. They were developed into a popular television series called *The Jersey*, which aired from 1999 to 2004.

## Early Achievements

No two people take the same path to success. Some people work very hard for a long time before achieving their goals. Others may take advantage of a fortunate turn of events. Biographers must make special note of the traits and qualities that allow their subjects to succeed.

**1** What was the person's most important early success?

**2** What process does the person use in his or her work?

**3** Which of the person's traits were most helpful in his or her work?

📖 In *Monday Night Football: Quarterback Exchange,* the main character trades places with football player John Elway. Elway played for the Denver Broncos, in the National Football League, from 1983 to 1998.

# Tricks of the Trade

Writing a story or a poem can be challenging, but it can also be very rewarding. Some writers have trouble coming up with ideas, while others have so many ideas that they do not know where to start. Gordon has special writing habits that young writers can follow to develop their ideas into great stories.

## Keep Your Eyes and Ears Open

Many writers get ideas by watching people and listening to conversations. If you pay attention, you will see that most people say and do all sorts of interesting things. Observing people can inspire writers to develop characters or to write funny scenes. Gordon has also said he often poses the question "what if?" and then comes up with ideas that could take place in real life, using his imagination to make his stories more interesting.

Authors get ideas from watching people and events around them. They incorporate what they see and hear into their stories.

## Write, Write, Write

Sometimes, the easiest way to finish a story is to write as much as possible in a first draft. This way, a writer can get all of his or her ideas down on paper. Then, the writer can decide which parts to keep. Very few writers have ever produced a great story in just one draft. Instead, they may review their first draft to see which parts should stay and what needs to be revised. Gordon says that 95 percent of what he knows about writing he learned from doing it.

> "The experience of *Island* (book series) has helped me with my humorous novels. *Island* showed me that a reader doesn't have to be in howling hysterics over every line."
> —*Gordon Korman*

## The Creative Process

Most writers have different opinions about the best time to write. Some work best late at night when everyone else is asleep. Others say that they are most productive early in the morning. There are also differing approaches to the writing process. Some writers need to make a detailed outline. This is a good idea for new writers, as it will help them to organize their thoughts. Some writers do not use an outline. They simply begin writing and let their ideas flow. Gordon says he likes to use an outline so he does not have to work as hard. He finds that writing without an outline can waste time and effort.

## It Takes Dedication

Writing takes dedication and discipline. Gordon writes eight hours every day. It takes him about six months to write a book, or a few months less than that for a series book, which already has established characters and settings. Gordon's willingness to work hard and his ability to tell great stories have led to many successful books.

Gordon often visits schools to talk about his books and the writing process with students.

# Remarkable Books

Gordon Korman is well known for his books for children and young adults. His stories have made readers laugh and have kept them in suspense. Here are some of Gordon's most popular books.

## The 39 Clues: One False Note

The reader's mission is to find 39 clues, hidden around the world in dangerous places, that hold the secret to the Cahill family's source of power. The Cahills are the most powerful family in the world. Some of the most influential people in history, including Benjamin Franklin, Amelia Earhart, and William Shakespeare, are members of the Cahill clan. Now the family has lost its power, and it needs the reader's help to get it back.

*One False Note* focuses on Wolfgang Amadeus Mozart, who is a Cahill and one of the world's most talented musicians ever. Fourteen-year-old Amy Cahill and her younger brother Dan trace Mozart's life through Vienna, Austria, as they follow a clue in a sheet of his music. Escaping police and a dangerous explosion, they find themselves navigating the canals of Venice, Italy, in their hunt for clues. *One False Note* is the second book of the first series and introduces readers to "the man in black."

***Titanic* Series**

**Book One: *Unsinkable***

**Book Two: *Collision Course***

**Book Three: *S.O.S.***

Facts dictate the fiction in Gordon's **trilogy** about the *Titanic*. History comes alive as readers follow four young passengers through the sailing and sinking of the newest, largest, and most luxurious ship of its time. Paddy is a stowaway, Sophie's mother is a **suffragette** from Boston, Juliana's father is a rich **eccentric,** and Alfie is hiding a secret that could get him kicked off the ship. A murderer is loose on the ship, and these characters find themselves tangled in a maze of mysteries, unaware of the icy and deadly danger that lies ahead.

This series was published in 2011, in time for the 100th anniversary of the ship's tragic end. After the "unsinkable" *Titanic* hit an iceberg on its maiden voyage in 1912, only 705 people out of the 2,228 on board were rescued.

## Liar, Liar, Pants On Fire

Zoe Bent, a little girl with a big imagination, did not stretch the truth for fun like her dad. She did it because she felt she had no choice. All the other third graders had cool stories to tell that were real. Zoe figured, when you are nobody special, you have to give the truth a little help. Making up one story after another, that is exactly what Zoe did.

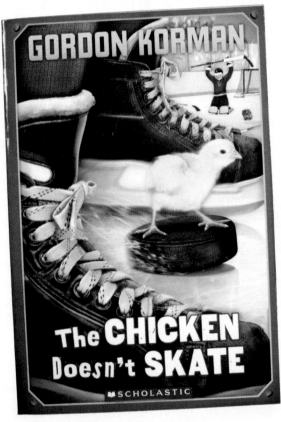

## The Chicken Doesn't Skate

Milo Neal's sixth grade science fair project, "The Complete Life Cycle of a Link in the Food Chain," takes an unexpected turn when a chicken named Henrietta, the focus of Milo's experiment, becomes the school hockey team's lucky mascot. Henrietta brings together an unlikely group of characters including a hockey star, a computer nerd, Milo, and an animal rights activist.

## This Can't Be Happening at Macdonald Hall!

*This Can't Be Happening At Macdonald Hall!* is Gordon's first book. Bruno and Boots, known for being troublemakers, were roommates at Macdonald Hall, a private school for boys. They stop being roommates when their troublemaking ways are discovered and the headmaster decides it would be best to separate the boys. This means Bruno must move in with the creepy Elmer Drimsdale and his ant colony. Boots does not fare much better when his new roommate turns out to be a nerd afraid of germs. This means war, and side-splitting comedy, as Bruno and Boots try to get their old room back.

## Showoff (Swindle Series #4)

Griffin Bing and his team of friends must figure out what to do after their guard dog, a Doberman named Luthor, injures a valuable show dog at a mall. Team member Samantha, who owns Luthor, is hit with a $7 million lawsuit, and Luthor is sent to the dog pound. Griffin gets Luthor released from the pound and makes a plan to turn the dog into a show dog. Luthor is entered as a competitor in a world show dog championship so the team can make enough money to pay off the lawsuit. Griffin and his friends enlist the help of a hilarious Russian dog trainer to get Luthor ready for the show. Meanwhile, the team also must solve the mystery of who is threatening to make sure Luthor loses the competition.

# From Big Ideas to Books

Gordon is a member of a team of authors involved in the exciting **multimedia** publishing project called *The 39 Clues*. The authors were given a basic plan for each book in the series. For example, Gordon knew that the second book in the series, *One False Note*, would start in Paris, because that is where the first book ended.

"I always start off with something real, but then I unleash my imagination to make it funnier, more interesting, and a better story."
—*Gordon Korman*

Readers of this series get to become a part of the story by accepting a mission and hunting for clues in books, game cards, and an online game. *The 39 Clues* is considered a groundbreaking concept in the world of publishing.

Gordon wrote two books and co-wrote a third for this project's first best-selling series. *Book 2: One False Note* and *Book 8: The Emperor's Code* were authored by Gordon. He co-wrote *Book 11: Vespers Rising* with three of the other authors working on the project.

## The Publishing Process

Publishing companies receive hundreds of manuscripts from authors each year. Only a few manuscripts become books. Publishers must be sure that a manuscript will sell many copies. As a result, publishers reject most of the manuscripts they receive. Once a manuscript has been accepted, it goes

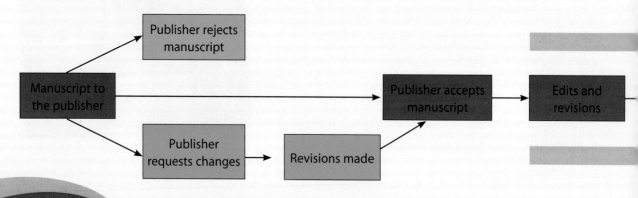

The first series was so popular that a second series was developed. Gordon was invited to create the first book for the next series. By being the first writer on the project, Gordon was able to set the stage for the rest of the writing team to follow. His book in the second series is called *The 39 Clues—Cahills vs. Vespers: The Medusa Plot*.

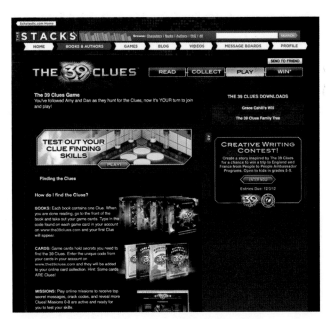

The 39 Clues series has grown. It now includes not only books, but cards and an online game as well.

through many stages before it is published. Often, authors change their work to follow an editor's suggestions. Once the book is published, some authors receive royalties. This is money based on book sales.

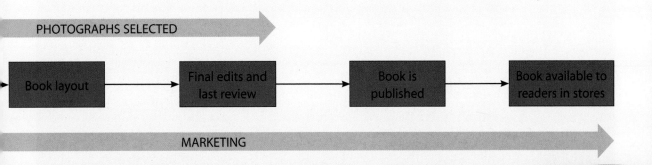

PHOTOGRAPHS SELECTED

Book layout → Final edits and last review → Book is published → Book available to readers in stores

MARKETING

# Gordon Korman Today

After university, Gordon stayed in New York. He married Michelle Iserson, an elementary school teacher from New York City. Together, they raise their family of three on Long Island, New York.

Gordon finds life is busy with his writing career. He usually has three projects underway at any given time, so he has to be well organized. One project will be in the writing stage, another in the editing stage, and a third in the planning stage. Once a book is published, it is distributed for sale. To help sell books, Gordon goes out to meet the public at presentations and book signings.

Gordon has more than 55 titles in print and has several more in the planning stages. He continues to write books for both children and young adults.

Gordon travels across North America to give school presentations about the writing process and the writing life. He answers questions, signs autographs, and talks about his newest books, including his **works in progress**. He often spends 40 days or more each year traveling to talk to fans and give presentations. Gordon's plans to write more in the future, including screenplays.

One reason Gordon's books are so popular is that he portrays young characters who obtain power and success in an adult world. He says that his favorite part of his career is getting paid for making things up, and he plans to do it for a long time. Gordon says he thinks of himself as the "Mick Jagger" of children's books. Mick Jagger is the lead singer of the band The Rolling Stones. The band still performs 50 years after being formed.

# Writing About the Person Today

The biography of any living person is an ongoing story. People have new ideas, start new projects, and deal with challenges. For their work to be meaningful, biographers must include up-to-date information about their subjects. Through research, biographers try to answer the following questions.

**1** Has the person received awards or recognition for accomplishments?

**2** What is the person's life's work?

**3** How have the person's accomplishments served others?

🐦 The Rolling Stones have been making music since 1962. They are one of the most respected bands in the music industry.

# Fan Information

Several of Gordon's books have won awards for literature in the children's and YA categories. However, his favorite awards are those given to him by his readers. Gordon has received a number of reader's choice awards for his books.

His first book, *This Can't Be Happening At Macdonald Hall!*, has been translated into French, Swedish, Danish, Norwegian, Chinese, Japanese, Portuguese, Italian, Korean, Dutch, and Greek. Now, children all over the world can enjoy Gordon's first published book. He has had other books translated into different languages, too.

Gordon launched the fourth novel in his Swindle series, *Showoff*, in 2012. The theme of this series is one that Gordon says he keeps returning to in his books. That theme is kids taking matters into their own hands when faced with problems. In the first Swindle book, the main character, Griffin Bing, is cheated out of a rare baseball card by an adult, and he sets out to get it back. In *Showoff*, Griffin Bing's gang helps turn a tough, mean attack dog into the world's top show dog.

Gordon went to New York's Westminster Kennel Club dog show to research *Showoff*. Westminster is one of the best-known dog shows in the world.

While Gordon continues to write new books, the popularity of his previous publications continues to grow. Movie producer Steven Spielberg was so impressed by *The 39 Clues* series that he bought the movie rights to it. *The 39 Clues: The Movie* is in development with a projected release date of 2014.

Another Korman book might also become a movie. *Ungifted*, a book scheduled for release in the fall of 2012, has been purchased by Walden Media, a children's film production company. *Ungifted* is about an average 14-year-old who ends up enrolled in a school for gifted students. The main character learns something about his own abilities while disrupting the routine of his peers at the uptight school.

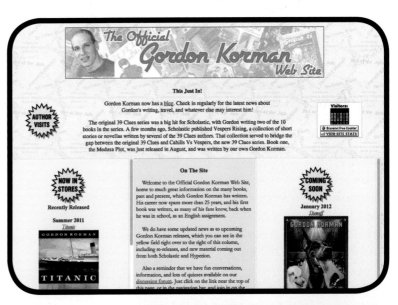

For all things Korman, the official Gordon Korman Web Site, at www.gordonkorman.com, has plenty of information. It even includes a blog by the Gordon himself.

Scholastic is Gordon's publisher. The site has information about the author and his books, including new releases, at www.scholastic.com.

At www.the39clues.com, readers can become part of the stories by cracking codes, hunting for clues, and completing a daring task.

# Write a Biography

A ll of the parts of a biography work together to tell the story of a person's life. Find out how these elements combine by writing a biography. Begin by choosing a person whose story fascinates you. You will have to research the person's life by using library books and the reliable websites. You can also email the person or write him or her a letter. The person might agree to answer your questions directly.

Use a concept web, such as the one below, to guide you in writing the biography. Answer each of the questions listed using the information you have gathered. Each heading on the concept web will form an important part of the person's story.

## Parts of a Biography

**Early Life**

Where and when was the person born?

What is known about the person's family and friends?

Did the person grow up in unusual circumstances?

**Growing Up**

Who had the most influence on the person?

Did he or she receive assistance from others?

Did the person have a positive attitude?

**Developing Skills**

What was the person's education?

What was the person's first job or work experience?

What obstacles did the person overcome?

**Person Today**

Has the person received awards or recognition for accomplishments?

What is the person's life's work?

How have the person's accomplishments served others?

**Early Achievements**

What was the person's most important early success?

What processes does this person use in his or her work?

Which of the person's traits were most helpful in his or her work?

# Test Yourself

**1** How old was Gordon Korman when he wrote his first book?

**2** Who does Gordon write his books for?

**3** Where was Gordon born?

**4** What series did he start with his first book?

**5** Where did Gordon grow up?

**6** What did Gordon study at university?

**7** *The Jersey* television series is based on a book series by Gordon. Which one?

**8** What type of writing is Gordon's favorite?

**9** What series did Gordon work on as a member of a team?

**10** Whom did Gordon marry, and what does she do?

# Writing Terms

The field of writing has its own language. Understanding some of the more common writing terms will allow you to discuss your ideas about books.

**action:** the events of a work of fiction

**antagonist:** the person in the story who opposes the main character

**autobiography:** a history of a person's life written by that person

**biography:** a written account of another person's life

**character:** a person in a story, poem, or play

**climax:** the most exciting moment or turning point in a story

**episode:** a short scene or piece of action in a story

**fiction:** stories about characters and events that are not real

**foreshadow:** hinting at something that is going to happen later in the book

**imagery:** a written description of a thing or idea that brings an image to mind

**narrator:** the person who relates the events of the story

**nonfiction:** writing that deals with real people and events

**novel:** published writing of considerable length that portrays characters within a story

**plot:** the order of events in a work of fiction

**protagonist:** the leading character of a story; often a likable character

**resolution:** the end of the story, when the conflict is settled

**scene:** a single episode in a story

**setting:** the place and time in which a work of fiction occurs

**theme:** an idea that runs throughout a work of fiction

# Key Words

**celebrity**: fame, a well-known person

**column**: a regular series of articles in a newspaper

**conceited**: having a very favorable opinion of yourself

**culture:** the beliefs, behaviors, objects, and other characteristics common to the members of a particular group

**eccentric:** an unconventional person

**juvenile fiction**: children's and youth, or young adult, fiction

**manuscript**: a book or document written by hand or typed

**multimedia**: something that uses multiple forms of media, such as online, print, film, sound recordings

**published**: printed for sale or given out to the public

**research**: to collect information on a subject

**screenplays**: scripts for films

**suffragette:** a woman seeking the right to vote through organized protest

**trilogy**: a set of three

**works in progress**: projects being worked on but not yet completed

# Index

# Log on to www.av2books.com

AV² by Weigl brings you media enhanced books that support active learning. Go to www.av2books.com, and enter the special code found on page 2 of this book. You will gain access to enriched and enhanced content that supplements and complements this book. Content includes video, audio, weblinks, quizzes, a slide show, and activities.

**Audio**
Listen to sections of
the book read aloud.

**Video**
Watch informative video clips.

**Embedded Weblinks**
Gain additional information
for research.

**Try This!**
Complete activities and
hands-on experiments.

# WHAT'S ONLINE?

|  Try This! |  Embedded Weblinks | Video | EXTRA FEATURES |
|---|---|---|---|
| Complete an activity about your childhood. | Learn more about Gordon Korman's life. | Watch a video about Gordon Korman. | |
| Try this timeline activity. | Learn more about Gordon Korman's achievements. | Watch this interview with Gordon Korman. | |
| See what you know about the publishing process. | Check out this site about Gordon Korman. | | |
| Test your knowledge of writing terms. | | | |
| Write a biography. | | | |

**Audio**
Listen to sections of
the book read aloud.

**Key Words**
Study vocabulary, and
complete a matching
word activity.

**Slide Show**
View images and captions,
and prepare a presentation.

**Quizzes**
Test your knowledge.

AV² was built to bridge the gap between print and digital. We encourage you to tell us what you like and what you want to see in the future.
**Sign up to be an AV² Ambassador at www.av2books.com/ambassador.**